Getting To Know...

Nature's Children

ORANGUTANS

Sheila Dalton

GROLIER
BOOKS

Facts in Brief

Classification of Orangutans

Class: *Mammalia* (mammals)

Order: *Primates* (apes, monkeys, lemurs, people)

Family: *Pongidae*

Genus: *Pongo*

Species: *Pongo pygmaeus*

World distribution. Today found only on the islands of Borneo and Sumatra in Southeast Asia.

Habitat. Rain forests.

Distinctive physical characteristics. Arms nearly twice as long as legs; hook-shaped hands and feet; long fur, usually reddish brown but sometimes darker; males grow fleshy cheek flaps, and both sexes have throat sacs.

Habits. Solitary; spend most of their time in trees; most build new nests to sleep in each night.

Diet. Mainly fruit.

This series is approved and recommended by the Federation of Ontario Naturalists.

Canadian Cataloguing in Publication Data

Dalton, Sheila
Gazelles; Orangutans

(Getting to know—nature's children)
ISBN 0-7172-2698-0

1. Gazelles—Juvenile literature.   2. Orangutan—Juvenile literature.
I. Title.   II. Title: Orangutans.   III. Series.

QL737.U53D35   1990a   j599.73'58   C90-095087-0

Have you ever wondered . . .

When you look at an orangutan's thoughtful eyes, smooth forehead and small, round ears, it's easy to see why it was given a name that means "person of the forest." Of the three great apes (gorillas, chimpanzees and orangutans) orangutans are the ones whose faces look the most like ours.

The resemblance is close enough that some people believe that the orangutan was actually created by mistake! According to a Malaysian legend, two bird gods made a man and a woman, then got so excited they partied all night. The next day, they weren't feeling too well. They tried to create some more humans, but they ended up with orangutans instead.

Life in the Forest

Opposite page:
The rain forest is the perfect place for a young orangutan to play hide-and-seek.

Many years ago, orangutans lived in dense jungles from South China to Java. Today they are found in the wild only on the two islands of Borneo and Sumatra in Southeast Asia.

Orangutans make their home in tropical rain forests. Heat, humidity, floods and gales are all part of life in these forests. Vegetation is thick, and the trees are tall. As much as 20 centimetres (8 inches) of rain may fall in a day.

The orangutan doesn't mind. It is used to the heat and rain. And up in tall trees is exactly where it prefers to spend its time.

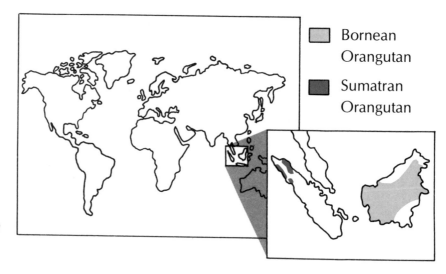

Bornean Orangutan

Sumatran Orangutan

The shaded areas on this map show where orangutans are found.

Up a Tree

Orangutans are the most arboreal of the great apes. That means they spend more of their time in trees than chimpanzees or gorillas do. They usually prefer to live near the middle of trees, but lightweight youngsters often venture up for a swing through the highest branches. Males occasionally travel on the ground, but females and babies rarely do.

An orangutan is well built for its life up in the trees. Its arms are nearly twice as long as its legs and reach down to its ankles when it stands upright. Its hands and feet are both hook-shaped — just what you need if you spend a lot of time swinging from branch to branch. As well, an orangutan's legs move as freely as its arms. In fact, it can even scratch its back with its toes!

But on the ground, the orangutan looks awkward and uncomfortable. It has to walk on the side of its feet since it cannot put them flat on the ground.

This young orangutan will grow to have an armspan of 2.4 metres (7.8 feet).

Safe and Dry

Like the other great apes, orangutans build nests up in the trees. About half an hour before sunset, which is orangutan bedtime, they pick a firm site in a fork or along a stout branch. Next, they gather lots of leafy branches and bend and twist them around one another to make a platform. Then they trample on them or pack them down with their fists, and maybe add some more broken branches and leaves to pad out the platform. To keep out the rain, they make a roof by piling leaves and twigs on overhanging branches. Or they may hold giant leaves, or big leafy branches, over their heads to act as umbrellas.

The whole task of nest making takes only about six minutes from start to finish. Most orangutans build a new nest each day, but they will return to an old one for a mid-morning nap or to sit out a rainstorm. At times, an adult male might build a nest on the ground or take a nap in a pile of leaves and twigs.

Female orangutans are very protective of their young.

Hilarious Headgear

Some scientists think the orangutan's habit of building a roof on its nest explains why it loves to put all sorts of things on its head. Others think that this behaviour may be a way of warding off stinging insects. Whatever the reason, the results can be very funny, especially when human and ape get together.

A Canadian anthropologist named Birute Galdikas lives in the rain forest of Borneo, where she often looks after orphaned baby orangutans until they are ready to cope on their own in the wild. Her young charges have been known to put anything from saucepans to potted plants on their heads. One even picked up Dr. Galdikas's pet kitten and plopped that down on its head. Talk about a furious feline!

A cosy roof of leaves.

Coat Tales

Not only do orangutans carry umbrellas, they also wear raincoats. That matted-looking mop of long reddish hair really does serve a purpose: it helps keep an orangutan's skin dry.

Actually, not all orangutans have the rusty-red fur we usually associate with them. Most do, but some of those on Borneo are maroon-tinted, and many older orangutans have chocolate-colored or almost black hair.

No matter what the shade, though, an orangutan's hair usually looks pretty messy. One reason may be that orangutans don't have anyone to groom their coats for them. Both chimpanzees and gorillas spend a lot of time grooming one another. Not so orangutans. Although females travel with their young and adolescents sometimes play together, most adults are such loners that they can go a month without seeing another orangutan.

Of course, orangutans pick dirt and insects off their skin, and mothers groom their babies. But beyond that, orangutans don't seem to notice— or care—how messy-looking their hair gets.

The Lone Ranger

There's a reason adult orangutans are such loners: they eat a lot of fruit. Fruit trees in the rain forest do not grow in clumps, but are widely scattered. If orangutans tried to stay in groups, several of them would be picking fruit off the same tree and there wouldn't be enough to go around. In fact, they'd have to find dozens of trees before everyone could be properly fed. And since orangutans are slow-moving creatures, they probably wouldn't get to enough trees in a day. An orangutan on its own, on the other hand, may only have to visit a few trees to eat its fill. In fact, if it finds a well-laden tree, one can be enough. Lone orangutans have been known to sit and feast all day in a single fruit tree.

As orangutans travel, they help the forest. The seeds of wild fruit pass through their digestive tracts and are deposited at some other place in the forest. Later, some of these seeds will grow into new fruit trees.

Dining alone again.

Food, Glorious Food

Orangutan's eat a lot because they are quite big. Although males grow only to a height of 1.5 metres (5 feet) — about the size of an average ten-year-old — they usually weigh between 50 and 90 kilograms (110-200 pounds). Females weigh somewhat more than half that and are 20 to 30 centimetres (8 to 12 inches) shorter. Both sexes eat mainly fruit.

Among other things, orangutans enjoy figs, plums and mangoes. For a bit of variety, they also snack regularly on bark, soil, leaves and insects, and treat themselves to an occasional bird's egg. But of the almost 400 varieties of food they eat, their favorite is a smelly, prickly, football-sized fruit called a durian.

Someone once said that a durian smells like a mixture of rotten eggs, onions and bad meat. Whew! Orangutans don't seem to mind the smell, though. They huff and smack their lips when munching on durians — ape-language for YUM!

A Bornean orangutan enjoys a leafy snack.

Elephants, Take Note

Orangutans have great memories. Once, an orangutan in a zoo discovered a weak spot in its cage and picked and picked at it. Finally, its keepers moved it to another cage. A year later, when it was returned to the original cage, it went right to the weak spot and started picking at it again.

Having a good memory helps the orangutan survive in the rain forest. Not only are the fruit trees there small and scattered, but some only produce fruit once every two or three years. And even then, the fruits don't ripen all at the same time. Without a good memory for time and place, orangutans could wear themselves out searching for food, and still they might not find enough. As it is, however, adult orangutans seem able to carry a map of their territory in their head, showing where each type of fruit grows — and when it will ripen.

So even though a typical orangutan brain is only one-third the size of yours, these hairy beasts are far from dumb.

Opposite page:
Orangutans don't drink much— sometimes they sip dew off plants or scoop out water trapped in holes in trees with their hands.

Good Senses

Not only are they smart, orangutans have excellent hearing and color vision. Because they don't have to fear many predators, they use their small, rounded ears mostly to listen for the calls of other orangutans. Good eyesight is helpful in finding fruit.

Since an orangutan sleeps for up to twelve hours at night, it doesn't need especially good night vision. And because it finds its food by memory and sight, it doesn't need (or have) a well-developed sense of smell. No wonder the rotten-smelling durian doesn't bother it at all!

An orangutan on the alert.

Tough Times

Life can look pretty easy for orangutans in the wild. They move slowly and rest a lot. In fact, an orangutan can spend over half a day napping.

But orangutans have their share of problems. They don't have to worry much about predators, but they suffer from broken bones and from fleas, ticks and other parasites. And they can catch human diseases such as pneumonia, malaria and polio.

Human beings are the orangutan's biggest problem. Sometimes people kill female orangutans so that they can capture their babies and sell them as pets or zoo animals. Logging and farming pose a threat, too; if the rain forest is cut down, the orangutan will have nowhere to live.

Solutions are being found, though. The governments of Borneo and Sumatra have made it illegal to capture or kill orangutans. And, all over the world, people are banding together to help save the rain forests.

"Wake me when it's time for dinner."

Face to Face

Many people think the world would be a poorer place without the "person of the forest." One of the many things that make the orangutan unique is its expressive face. Although they look like one another at first glance, it is really quite easy to tell individual orangutans apart. Their facial features, like ours, can vary a lot — more than those of the other great apes.

Bornean and Sumatran orangutans have slightly different faces. The Sumatran orangutan has a long, oval face. The Bornean's is thicker and broader. Both types have facial hair, but the Sumatran male grows a much fuller beard and mustache than the Bornean male.

There is another difference. Adult males of both types have big, fat cheeks — but the Bornean's grow so big, he can barely see around them!

It's hard to believe, but in the matter of cheek flaps, this Sumatran orangutan is outdone by his Bornean cousin.

Flap, Flap, I Love You

Scientists are not sure why male orangutans develop such fat faces, but they think those fleshy flaps might actually make a male more attractive to females that are ready to mate. Fat cheeks might also be a handy source of nourishment. When food is scarce, the orangutan's body could possibly use the fat stored in its cheeks to survive until more tasty fare becomes available.

Both males and females develop throat sacs that serve much the same purpose as the amplifier on your stereo, making the orangutan's calls louder. Males have particularly impressive pouches and can blow them up like giant balloons when they want to let the world know they're around.

A thoughtful moment.

The Long Call

When a male orangutan blows up his throat pouch and lets rip, he is making what is known as the "long call." This tremendous sound can last anywhere from two to four minutes. It usually starts with a low rumble, turns into a noise like a trumpeting elephant, then ends with long sighs. Some people who have heard it say the whole thing sounds like one huge burp! However you describe it, it is loud enough to be heard from a kilometre or so (over half a mile) away.

The long call is used mainly to warn other males to stay out of an orangutan's territory, but it comes in handy for attracting females, too. It is also useful for locating other orangutans in the forest. Although they are solitary, orangutans like to keep tabs on one another's whereabouts.

Orangutans make a dozen or more other sounds, including a warning "bark." And females use a particular call described as a "kiss-squeak" to express annoyance with a male's unwelcome attentions.

"Don't come any closer!"

Enter at Your Own Risk

Many male orangutans claim a territory of about 5 square kilometres (2 square miles). Several females usually live within this area on overlapping home ranges of about 100 hectares (250 acres) each. Females limit their movement to an area just big enough to feed themselves and their offspring. Males travel farther afield, looking for mates in addition to food.

A male uses the long call to protect his territory, and if that doesn't work, he indulges in a show of strength called a display. He does this by ripping branches from trees and throwing them on the ground or shaking them furiously. He also inflates his throat pouch and makes threatening grunting noises.

When two adult males meet, they often display, but they seldom fight. The male who is trespassing on the other's territory usually gives in fairly soon. If they do fight, it will likely be over a female who is ready to mate.

Despite their threatening appearance, male orangutans rarely fight.

Getting Together

A female orangutan can mate when she is 7 years old, but often she will wait until she is 10 or 11 to take a partner. After she has a baby, she will not mate again until the largest part of child-rearing is over. This takes at least four years and sometimes it may be eight or nine years before the female mates again. For this reason, and since the female almost always has only one baby at a time, the orangutan population grows slowly.

A male can mate when he is 10, but he often has to wait. Females seem to prefer bigger males, between 12 and 15 years old. These are the males who have fought for and won their own territory. They are the strongest males around, and so should father the strongest, healthiest offspring.

"Mom, listen to how loud I can yell!"

Hang On There, Baby

Nine months after mating, the female gives birth in her nest in a tree. The newborn orangutan weighs between one and two kilograms (two and four pounds) and is usually covered with orange fur. Its brown face has light areas around the eyes and mouth, which will darken as it grows older.

The new mother stays in the nest with her baby for at least a week, until it is old enough to travel. As soon as it can hang on tightly to her fur, she's on the move again. Then Junior is in for a safe but bumpy ride, as mother and baby swing through the trees together.

Sometimes it's exhausting being a young orangutan.

Super Mom

Female orangutans make very good mothers. They protect their babies from danger and hug and snuggle, just as your mom did when you were little. Sometimes they play games, like tickle-your-toes and hide-and-seek, with their young.

Many young orangutans cling to their mother almost continually until they are around a year and a half old. They drink her milk, and they ride on her body and share her nest for at least three years, and sometimes they stay with her for as many as six or seven years. A mother orangutan cleans her baby's fur and keeps its fingernails short with her teeth. She also washes it with rain water.

It's difficult to believe that this nearly naked 6-week-old orangutan will one day be as large and hairy as its mother.

Acting Like A Baby

In some ways, baby orangutans are a lot like human babies. They cry when they are hungry or uncomfortable. They seek affection from Mom by climbing into her lap or nuzzling and snuggling up to her. They also have a wide range of emotions. They get sad, happy and angry. Once, a mother orangutan was a bit slow to share a mango with her little one. The baby threw a temper tantrum — squealing and jumping up and down in rage. Mom ignored the racket for a while, then calmly handed her offspring a slice as if nothing unusual had happened.

Compared with human babies, however, baby orangutans show little interest in language or tools. In fact, they show little interest in anything but food!

"Which one should I eat first?"

Lessons from Mom

The young orangutan learns how to take care of itself slowly and steadily. First, it figures out what's good to eat — and what's not — by watching Mom. Mom plays a more active role when it comes to climbing and walking. She pushes her youngster out on branches, or leaves it alone on the ground, so that it has no choice but to learn how to get around on its own.

By the time they are four, most orangutan youngsters can select their own food, swing through the trees on their own and make nests. They still choose to sleep with Mom at night, but they are getting more and more able to take care of themselves.

Going It Alone

When its mother has a new baby, the young orangutan finds itself pushed out of the family nest. At first, it doesn't like this at all! It tries to get back in, and Mom may have to smack and even bite it before it will go away and build its own nest.

For a while, the youngster hangs around its mother and the new baby during the day and nests close to them at night. It may even entertain the new baby now and then with games of peek-a-boo. Then, one day, it may meet up with some other adolescent orangutans and wander off with them — the first step to a life on its own.

With luck, and if its habitat is not destroyed, the young orangutan can look forward to anywhere from 40 to 60 years of swinging through the rain forest.

Special Words

Ape   Group of animals that includes gorillas, chimpanzees, orangutans, gibbons and siamangs. The first three are known as the great apes.

Arboreal   That lives in trees.

Display   A noisy performance a male orangutan puts on to scare away other males.

Durian   A foul-smelling but pleasant-tasting fruit particularly favored by orangutans.

Groom   To clean or brush, especially hair.

Home range   Area through which an animal moves in search of food.

Long call   Name given to particularly loud call made by male orangutans and lasting two to four minutes.

Parasite   Organism that grows and feeds on the body of another. Fleas and ticks are parasites.

Rain forest   Densely forested area that receives over 250 centimeters (100 inches) of rain a year.

Territory   Area that an animal or a group of animals lives in and often defends from other animals of the same kind.

INDEX

Cover Photo: Dede Gilman (Unicorn Stock Photos)

Photo Credits: Bill Ivy, pages 4, 24, 36; Kjell B. Sandved, pages 7, 12; Evelyn Gallardo, page 8; Douglas T. Cheeseman, Jr., page 11; Louie Bunde (Unicorn Stock Photos), pages 15, 32; Tom McHugh (Photo Researchers, Inc.), page 16, 27, 40; Boyd Norton, page 19, 44; Nancy Adams, pages 20, 23; Four By Five, pages 28, 43; Alice Taylor (Photo Researchers, Inc.), page 31; Shostal Associates, page 35; Nancy Staley, pages 38, 39.

Getting To Know...

Nature's Children

GAZELLES

Sheila Dalton

GROLIER
BOOKS

Facts in Brief

Classification of Gazelles

Class: *Mammália* (mammals)

Order: *Artiodactyla*

Family: *Bovidae*

Genus: *Gazella;* several antelopes of other genera are also commonly considered gazelles.

Species: There are about 12 species of gazelles.

World distribution. Mongolia and India to Egypt and Morocco and into eastern and central tropical Africa.

Habitat. Open plains, mountains and bush.

Distinctive physical characteristics. Slender body and long thin legs with two-toed hoofs. In most species male and female have black-ringed horns. Coat is brown with white underside and rump, and black and white markings on face. Ears are long and narrow, and tail is short.

Habits. Gazelles often graze in herds of up to several hundred. They are very fast runners.

Diet. Grass, herbs, leaves and roots.

This series is approved and recommended by the Federation of Ontario Naturalists.

Canadian Cataloguing in Publication Data

Dalton, Sheila
  Gazelles; Orangutans

(Getting to know—nature's children)
ISBN 0-7172-2698-0

1. Gazelles—Juvenile literature.   2. Orangutan—Juvenile literature.
I. Title.   II. Title: Orangutans.   III. Series.

QL737.U53D35 1990a   j599.73'58   C90-095087-0

Have you ever wondered . . .

Everyone agrees that gazelles are among the world's most graceful animals, but did you know that they are also very, very fast? Some can reach speeds of over 80 kilometres (50 miles) an hour for 15 seconds or more. That's as fast as a car on a highway.

And did you know that gazelles belong to a group of animals known as antelopes? That won't surprise you if you know that the word antelope means bright-eyed, since a gazelle's large shining eyes are one of its most striking features.

To find out more about this beautiful and surprisingly hardy animal, just turn the page.

Addra gazelle.

Where They Live

Opposite page:
The unusual coloring on the face and long straight horns identify this animal as a Thomson's gazelle.

Gazelles are found in Asia and Africa. Some make their home in mountainous regions, others in the desert or in shrubby areas known as the bush. Most live on grassy plains.

Whatever the area gazelles call home, it is always an open one, with very few places to hide. Often rain is seasonal, so at certain times of the year water is scarce. Fortunately, some gazelles — the Moroccan Dorcas, for instance — do not need to drink water at all.

They get the moisture they need from the roots and plants they eat.

Other gazelles are not so lucky. They do need to drink, and they depend on their speed and endurance to travel great distances to whatever watering holes they can find.

The shaded area on this map shows where gazelles are found.

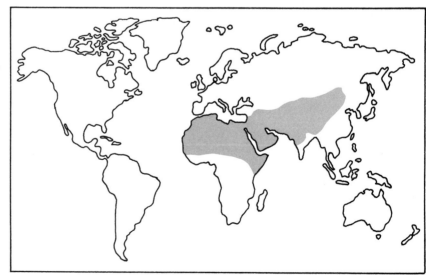

Big and Little

There are at least ten different kinds of gazelles and some zoologists list as many as eighteen. Most have sandy brown coats with white undersides and rumps. Many have black and white markings on their faces and a horizontal dark band along each side. Their long pointed ears and large eyes give them a gentle appearance. Most have long V- or S-shaped horns.

The smallest gazelle is the Dorcas gazelle. It is not much bigger than a medium-sized dog, averaging 53 centimetres (21 inches) at the shoulder. The largest is the Dama gazelle, which is about the size of a Great Dane. But the gazelle's long neck, long horns and long, slender legs make it look much taller.

The small yet elegant Dorcas gazelle.

Groups of Gazelles

Generally speaking, gazelles live in herds. Although a male, or buck, will wander alone at times, he is usually trying to establish a territory. Then he will mark out a large area of land as his own, and be joined by a group of females, or does. Usually, these females do not stay very long, but they are soon replaced by a new group. When a herd of does stay with a male longer than a few days, it is known as a harem. But harems move on too after a few weeks or months. Does and their young make up another kind of herd. Bachelors, too, hang around together. There are also mixed groups of both sexes and all ages. These usually form outside the breeding season and can range in size from three to ten thousand or more.

The horns of these Grant's gazelles may grow to be as long as these animals are tall.

Gazelle Grub

Gazelles are browsers and grazers. This means that sometimes they eat grass, herbs and woody plants on the ground (graze), and sometimes they munch on the leaves, buds and shoots of trees and shrubs (browse). Some may also use their hoofs to dig up roots.

Just like other antelopes, and even cows, gazelles are ruminants, or cud-chewers. They swallow their food mainly unchewed and then bring it back to their mouth later to chew it more thoroughly. This allows them to eat quickly wherever they can find food — maybe under the watchful eye of a predator. Then they can chew it at their leisure afterwards, somewhere safer.

To reach an out-of-the-way treat this gerenuk simply stands on its back legs and stretches its long neck.

Tibetan gazelle

Dama gazelle

Goitered gazelle

Horns-a-Plenty

One of the first things you notice about a gazelle is its magnificent set of horns.

A gazelle's horns are usually long, pointed and slender, with thickenings that form black rings at regular intervals. They can be straight, or curved forward or back, but they never have branches. Unlike a deer whose antlers are shed every year and replaced with a new set, a gazelle keeps its horns throughout its life. The core of the horn is an outgrowth of bone that begins at the gazelle's skull. The core is covered in keratin — the same stuff that your fingernails are made of. One of the most amazing things about a gazelle's horns is that they never stop growing.

In African gazelles, both males and females usually have horns. The female's horns are often shorter and thinner than those of the male, however. In most Asian gazelles, only the male has horns.

The springbuck is a beautiful gazelle with curving horns, long ears and large eyes surrounded by long lashes.

When Push Comes to Shove

Although a gazelle's horns can look fairly threatening, they are seldom actually used as weapons. Male gazelles mostly use them to show off, as if to say, "Hey, look at my horns! Aren't they something?" Often that's all it takes to scare off a rival. Even when two males do fight, they seldom hurt each other, and unless the fight is over a female, there is often no obvious winner or loser. The two bucks just lock horns, and push and twist and shove until one breaks away. Then one or both of them will just switch to another activity. A fight usually lasts no longer than five minutes, and is sometimes as short as a few seconds.

Gazelle fighting, in fact, is sometimes so tame that the opponents may not even touch each other at all! In "air-cushion-fighting," they face each other at a distance of a metre (yard) or two, go through all the motions of fighting, but never come into contact.

Just letting off a bit of steam.

Gazelle Horns

Slender-horned gazelle

Dibatag

Blackbuck

Putting on a Show

Gazelle males rarely need to fight because they have other ways of letting one another know who's boss. A territorial male with a harem will often separate himself from the females, moving and grazing apart from them. This allows other males to see him from a distance. That's usually enough to keep them off his property.

When bucks do meet, the older or territorial one may do a number of things to tell the other "I'm in charge around here." For instance, he'll lift his nose so high his horns touch his back, or he'll turn his head quickly to one side. If this doesn't work, lowering his horns as if he's ready to fight does the trick. The younger or non-territorial male almost always backs down, dropping to his knees with head and neck stretched forward. Then he gets up and calmly goes about his business. He may not leave the territory, but for the time being at least, he will not try to take it away from its owner.

A male gazelle on the watch as his harem feeds.

Staking Out a Territory

There comes a time in all male gazelles' lives when they feel the urge to establish their own territory. Many young bucks find and take over a territory that has been left vacant. In some species, a male seeks out a group of does and simply moves in. But sometimes a young buck must fight an older male in order to win his territory. Whoever loses has to move on.

You would think that after finding a place to call his own, a buck would hang on to it. But often he doesn't. He may just stop being territorial one day, sometimes after as little as two months. In some cases, the females move out and the buck is left alone. He may then join a mixed herd or a group of wandering bachelors before establishing a territory again later. Many bucks repeat this cycle several times.

However short-lived, territoriality serves a purpose. The male provides protection for does and young. He also has many females to mate with. This means that more strong young are born, which helps the species to survive.

A trio of Grant's gazelles on the alert.

Home on the Range

Once he's on his own turf, a buck has a rather odd way of making himself at home. He goes to the middle of his territory and drops some dung. He does this every day until quite a heap has formed. This seems to be his version of putting up a sign with his name on it.

Bucks also mark their territories with urine, and in many species they use glands just beneath their eyes as well. These glands are called the preorbital glands. A buck will carefully lower his head until the gland comes into contact with a blade of grass, depositing a secretion that hardens in the open air. Does have these glands, too, but only the males mark objects with them.

Sometimes a passing male will sniff the mark, then leave one of his own nearby — a kind of calling card to say he's stopped by. All these marking behaviors help the buck become familiar with his territory, while at the same time keeping him in communication with other males.

You can tell this Dorcas gazelle is a young one because its horns are quite small and it has not yet acquired the striking colors of the adults.

Cool, Calm and Collected

Overleaf:
*Roosevelt's
gazelles.*

For an animal that seems to go out of its way to avoid a fight, gazelles have a lot of enemies. Lions, leopards, hyenas, cheetahs and wild dogs hunt and kill adult gazelles. In Asia, wolves are a major danger. Pythons can swallow small gazelles whole, after wrapping themselves around them and cutting off their breathing. Jackals, baboons and tawny eagles also prey upon fawns.

With all these dangers to face, you'd expect gazelles to be a nervous bunch. But they actually live and eat very peacefully. A herd will get upset if one of them is captured and killed, but it quickly settles down again. And gazelles do not even react to a predator unless it is really a threat. If a lion passes by, for instance, the herd will pay no attention to it at all unless it is obvious that the lion is hunting and going to attack. This way, the gazelles save energy for those times when they do have to run for their lives.

A Friend in Need

An animal with so many enemies needs good friends as well — and luckily, gazelles have some.

East African oxpeckers, a kind of starling, prowl the bodies of gazelles in search of ticks, maggots and bloodsucking flies. They even clean up any open wounds a gazelle may have. Gazelles can often be seen turning their heads and holding their ears steady so that an oxpecker can reach in and peck out a bug or two. And when danger threatens, the oxpecker always runs to the side facing away from the enemy before flying away. This alerts the gazelle to the direction in which danger is approaching.

Zebras and giraffes often share feeding areas and watering holes with gazelles. They help each other because they have different strengths. Although gazelles have good eyesight, zebras and giraffes can spot an enemy before they can. On the other hand, gazelles have keener noses and sharper ears, and they smell or hear danger before either of the other two.

Opposite page:
The giraffe is a friendly watchtower for any nearby gazelles, alerting them to dangers only it can see far in the distance.

Keeping Out of Trouble

A gazelle is actually well protected against danger. In addition to super senses, it has a coat that blends in with its surroundings, making it hard for an enemy to see.

Some gazelles with striped flanks shake them before running away from an enemy. This warns the rest of the herd of danger. Others lift up their tails in a flash of white, and some sound the alarm with a loud snort. This tells nearby gazelles to stop everything and run.

Generally, gazelles are not strong enough to fight their enemies. Their best defense is to run. But instead of running in a straight line, they zigzag. That way, the predator never knows where they're headed next. Gazelles have even been seen jumping straight over lions that were rushing right at them.

The Thomson's gazelle is one of the most common animals of eastern Africa's plains.

Spotted and Stotted

Gazelles have another very clever way of dealing with enemies. It's called stotting, and it works so well that it's one big reason they don't need to run away whenever a predator appears.

Stotting refers to a gazelle's way of leaping high in the air with its legs stiff and its back arched. Zoologists now think that this strange bouncing behavior is gazelle-talk for "You've been spotted. Don't bother trying to sneak up on me." Most predators know that healthy gazelles can outrun them. If they can't surprise one, they won't bother chasing it.

They might, however, give chase to an old or weak gazelle, and stotting may transmit another message as well: "See how fit and strong I am!" If the predator had any thought of being able to win a race with this gazelle, it now knows it is hopelessly outmatched.

Stotting springbuck

"Run!"

Helpful Herds

When it comes to safety and protection, the herd itself serves a useful function. In a herd, there is always someone acting as a look-out. A herd has hundreds, sometimes thousands, of eyes, ears and noses to help spot an enemy. Also, it is hard for a predator to isolate a single animal in a herd. In a mass of animals, a hungry lion or wild dog has less room to move about and is hampered in its attack. A victim can escape by mingling in the crowd.

Moreover, predators always direct their attack against a single animal. But the herd makes this difficult to do. When a predator charges, the herd bursts out in all directions and the chosen victim disappears in the crowd. The enemy, its movements hampered by the milling mass of animals, gets confused and wastes time trying to home in on it again. Lions, in particular, are easily distracted this way. Unfortunately, cheetahs seem to be able to concentrate on one animal in a herd no matter what the others are doing.

Safety in numbers.

Starting a Family

Gazelles mate all year round. Different species have different peak periods. For example, some gazelles breed so that most of the young are born during the rainy season, when food and water are plentiful.

To attract a doe's attention, a buck will put on a courtship display — he lifts his nose in the air and kicks his front legs straight out in front of him, like a soldier on parade. Sometimes, he puts his legs right under the female's belly. He'll also sniff her urine. If she is ready to mate, her urine has a certain smell only a male gazelle can appreciate.

If all goes well, she and the buck will then perform a mating march, with the doe in the lead. Mating itself is brief and, soon afterwards, the two go their separate ways.

"Let's get acquainted."

Birth of a Fawn

About five to seven months after mating, depending on the species, the doe gives birth to a single baby, or fawn. In some species, the male stays close by her after the birth — but not because of the baby. He's really hoping to persuade the female to mate with him again.

Right after birth, the mother gazelle cleans her baby by licking it all over, from its head to its hoofs. She may be labeling the fawn with her own scent this way, so that she can find it again. For she will soon leave it on its own and rejoin the herd for a short while.

The licking also has a kind of "waking up" effect on the fawn. Within minutes, it struggles to its feet — sometimes with a helpful prod, or even a kick, from Mom. After it has nursed for a little while, it will move away to find a hiding place where its tawny coat blends in with its surroundings. There it will bed down until its mother calls it again for more nursing.

A newborn gazelle gets a loving lick from its mother.

Practice Makes Perfect

The new baby will stay hidden for at least the first two weeks of its life. When Mom comes to nurse it, it will answer her cries and come out from its hiding place to meet her. Then, sometimes after a bit of nose-nuzzling, it settles down for a good meal.

After feeding comes playtime. The fawn bounces around its mother in circles, stopping only when it has to catch its breath. Then it starts all over again. At last it's had enough, and totters off to its hiding place.

As the fawn gets a little older, it sometimes plays at fighting. When its mother approaches, it lowers its head. If Mom then lowers hers in response to this "threat," the fawn scampers around in delight, carried away with the fun of it all. Without realizing it, the youngster is learning and practicing for when it grows up.

Staying well hidden until its mother calls.

Don't Mess with Mom

When it's about two to three weeks old, the young gazelle starts following its mother for longer and longer periods, slowly becoming a full-fledged member of the herd. That's when the doe's protective instincts really come into their own. Any predator that threatens her baby had better watch out! Normally gentle, mother gazelles have been known to attack jackals and baboons. One was even seen chasing a baboon for three hours after it had killed her fawn. A gazelle mom will sometimes charge people, too, if they get too close to her offspring.

Usually, though, gazelle moms will try to distract an enemy rather than attack it. When a fawn is too young to run fast, it will hide from a predator while its mother and other adults in the herd flee. This distracts the animal from the baby. Because adult gazelles run so fast, often nobody gets hurt.

This young Saharan Dorcas gazelle will not be nursing for much longer. It's getting to be too big.

Adolescence

A young gazelle usually nurses for about four to six months. What seems to bring nursing to an end is the size of the fawn. Before, when it butted its head into its mother's belly to get the milk flowing, no harm was done. But now it's big enough to hurt and Mom starts avoiding it at feeding time.

Still, the two will stay together in the same herd for the time being. Soon, though, a young male may find himself being harassed by the adult buck that owns the territory. Clearly, the time has come for him to leave and join a bachelor herd. A young female often stays with her mother's herd at least until she is old enough to seek a mate of her own, usually when she is about 18 months old.

Looking into the Future

In order for gazelles to continue to survive in Asia and Africa, people must make an effort to provide safe places for them to live. Right now, many of them are being killed by hunters and more and more of their grazing land is being turned into farms. Fortunately, efforts are being made by governments and individuals to protect the gazelle. Game reserves and national parks have been set up in many of the countries where they live, and the future is beginning to look brighter for these beautiful and graceful animals.

Special Words

Antelopes   A group of hoofed, cud-chewing mammals that includes gazelles.

Antler   Branched bony growth on the heads of deer and their relatives. Antlers are shed each year.

Breeding season   The time of the year during which animals come together to produce young.

Browse   Feed on leaves and shoots of trees and shrubs.

Buck   A male gazelle.

Cud   Hastily swallowed food brought back for chewing by animals such as gazelles, deer and cows.

Doe   A female gazelle.

Fawn   A young gazelle.

Gland   An organ of the body where certain substances are made.

Graze   Feed on grass and plants on the ground.

Harem   Herd of female gazelles that gathers and stays some time in a male's territory.

Horn   A bony outgrowth on the head of gazelles, other antelopes, sheep, cattle and goats. Horns are not shed and continue to grow throughout the animal's life.

Keratin   Protein that forms the basis of horns, nails, feathers, hair and scales.

Predator   An animal that hunts other animals for food.

Ruminant   An animal that chews the cud, including antelopes, cows, sheep and camels.

Stotting   A high stiff-legged jump characteristic of gazelles. Also called *pronking*.

Territory   Area that an animal or group of animals lives in and often defends from other animals of the same kind.

INDEX

Cover Photo: Stephen J. Krasemann (Peter Arnold, Inc.)
Photo Credits: Zoological Society of San Diego, pages 4, 24, 25, 43; Steven C. Kaufman (Peter Arnold, Inc.), page 7; John Newby (WWF-Photolibrary, page 8; Breck P. Kent, pages 11, 16; Stan Bain, page 12; Phyllis Greenberg, pages 15, 35; Gerald & Buff Corsi, pages 19, 31, 36; Sandved & Coleman Photography, pages 20, 32; Nancy Adams, page 23; Bill Ivy, page 27; Barry Dursley, page 28; Klaus Paysan (Peter Arnold, Inc.), page 39; George W. Frame (WWF-Photolibrary), page 40.